My Little Book of

Bald Eagles

By Hope Irvin Marston
Illustrated by Stephanie Mirocha

Windward Publishing
AN IMPRINT OF FINNEY COMPANY
www.finneyco.com

One early spring morning two bald eagles returned to their gigantic nest high above a large lake. They had hatched their young there for ten years. They repaired the winter damage with small branches and twigs. Then they spiraled down to the ground to gather moss and leaves.

>rustle!<
>rustle!<
>rustle!<

The female scratched about to make a soft place to lay her eggs. She hollowed out a spot and treaded the moss and leaves in place to line it.

The eagle rested for
a moment. Then, far below,
she spied a silvery fish
near the surface of
the lake.

SWOOP!

In a blink she dropped down and snatched it
with her talons. She carried it to a nearby tree
and perched on a branch.

With her beak she tore off chunks of fish and swallowed them.

The next morning the eagles flew high in the air.
They *dove* and *chased* each other playfully.
They courted by locking their talons
in the air. They spun downward.
Before hitting the ground,
they let go.

TWIRL and SWIRL

Up they swooped again, and then spiraled down once more.

TWIRL and SWIRL

A few days later the female laid an off-white egg in her soft nest. Two days after that she laid a second one. She sat on the nest to keep her eggs warm and safe from gulls and crows. Now and then she turned them.

She had been sitting in the nest for a week. She wanted to leave it and go fishing.

Her mate balled his claws, straddled the eggs, and settled down over them.

Chitter! Chitter!

SCRATCH! SCRATCH!
In about five weeks, the first chick tried to get out of his shell. He pipped it with an "egg tooth" on his tiny beak.

CRACK!

A day later the tired little eaglet broke out. He spent the day sleeping under his mother. The next day his mother fed him tiny bits of fish.

The second eaglet hatched two days later.

>peck!< >peck!<

>peck!<

The baby birds ate often and grew quickly.
Within three weeks they were each a foot tall,
and their beaks and feet were almost full grown.

One adult stayed in the nest with them, shielding them from weather and other birds.

At six weeks the eaglets were nearly as tall as their parents. They trudged around their huge nest.

They flapped their wings in the wind. They hopped and wiggled and *s t r e t c h e d.*

Their mother brought a catfish to the nest. The eaglets watched her stand on the fish and tear it apart. When she moved away, they ripped the pieces into bite-sized bits and swallowed them.

At nine weeks, the growing eaglets teetered on the edge of the nest. They flapped their wings in the breeze.

~Chirp!~

~Chirp!~

~Chirp!~

They were not
yet ready to take
their first big leap
from the nest.

A few weeks later, the older eaglet lifted his wings and a puff of wind carried him into a nearby tree. He landed so fast that he almost fell to the ground.

Later that day, the younger
bird fledged on her own.
She reached for her
intended perch,
but missed it.

As the fledgling
eagles practiced flying,
they avoided crashing
into branches.
At times they
barely missed
hitting power lines.
They grew stronger.
They learned quickly.
They made fewer mistakes.

Their parents still brought
food back to the nest for them.

They needed to learn
to fish on their own.

The young eagles watched their father swoop down over the lake. He speared a fish with his talons and flew up to a tree to eat it.

ZING!

The youngsters tried to do the same thing. At first they snagged only dead fish.

Soon they learned to catch live ones, which tasted better.

After the lake froze, they migrated
to open water with other young eagles.

They spent the winter along a *flowing* river where they would find plenty of fish.

During the next four years the eagles moved from place to place. They lost their dark brown feathers in their first annual molt.

The following year their feathers lightened.
A few white ones appeared on their bellies.

By the time they were five years old,
the birds had become adults.

The feathers on their heads and tails had turned snowy white. Their bodies were covered with thousands of feathers.

They found mates, built nests near where they had hatched, and raised families of their own.

When winter drew near, the eagles left
their nesting area in search of open water.
With skill and luck, these majestic
monarchs of the sky could live
another thirty years.

How awesome to watch them
mount the wind and soar above
the earth—forever flying free.

DEDICATIONS:

FOR ALL THE AMERICAN EAGLE HEROES WHOSE CONTRIBUTIONS AND HARD WORK HELPED BRING THE BALD EAGLE BACK FROM THE BRINK OF EXTINCTION.
— H.I.M.

FOR ERLING AND SONIA.
— S.M.

AUTHOR'S NOTE:

Bald eagles are a protected species. There are stiff penalties for anyone caught bothering them. When eagles are found dead—from collisions with cars, being unlawfully shot or trapped, or from natural causes—the U.S. Fish and Wildlife Service salvages them. American Indians can legally acquire eagle feathers from this organization for use in religious ceremonies. For additional information about bald eagles, including live nesting pictures each spring, visit the American Eagle Foundation's Web site at www.eagles.org.

ACKNOWLEDGMENTS:

The author wishes to thank Robert M. Hatcher, Eagle Consultant, American Eagle Foundation, for his generous help in checking the text for accuracy and completeness.

The illustrator would like to thank Dr. Patrick T. Redig, Professor of Avian Medicine and Surgery at the University of Minnesota, co-founder and former director of the University of Minnesota Raptor Center for sharing his expertise in bald eagle behavior and habitat. She would also like to acknowledge the National Eagle Center in Wabasha, Minnesota, and Aitkin High School.

Copyright © 2009 Hope Irvin Marston
Illustrations Copyright © 2009 Stephanie Mirocha

ISBN 13: 978-0-89317-068-4

This book is part of the My Little Book collection. For other titles in this collection, visit www.finneyco.com or your favorite bookseller.

Printed in the United States of America

Windward Publishing

8075 215th Street West
Lakeville, Minnesota 55044
AN IMPRINT OF FINNEY COMPANY
www.finneyco.com